WEALTH BUILDING

WIZARDS

The Art and Science of Smart Investing

Jasmine Kevin

Table of Contents

CHAPTER ONE

INTRODUCTION

Expecting that your hold stays aware of goal is more than five years away, setting a piece of your cash into hypotheses could get your money go further and help you with remaining mindful of widening costs. How do speculations function?

Undertakings are investments or purchases made with cash. A different group looks at four basic types of hypotheses that are completely settled on things they all have in common. Resource classes" recommend these:

Shares: Purchasing a stake in an association;

Cash: save keeps up with in a bank or building society account;

Property: making an interest in a private or business building; In addition, fixed pay protections, also known as securities, are IOUs that are offered in exchange for a cash credit to a company or organization.

Monetary: A monetary partner's portfolio is an assortment of their different assets. As a last resort, parting your money between the different resource classes diminishes the general bet of your portfolio by forgetting to differentiate speculations and later failing with do thusly.

There are different undertaking structures. Different people contribute through complete or 'pooled' resources, for instance, unit trusts.

Returns

Returns are the advantage you secure from your endeavors. It might be paid for in various ways, dependent upon how much money you have:

Benefits (from shares);

Lease (from properties);

Premium (from cash stores and fixed-pay affirmations);

Contrast (capital developments or tortures) between the cost you address and the cost you sell for. With a subsequent access cash account you can take out cash whenever you like and it's beginning and end saw as seen as a safeguarded try. It is likely that the value of the money invested in fixed-interest securities, shares, or real estate will fluctuate over time, but it should grow more over time. Taking everything into account, each project will probably be successful in some other way.

HOW COSTS DECLINE EXPERIENCE RETURNS PLANNING

Projects calls for investment and cash, and expert connections, for example, store the stack up affiliations, will charge an expense. You can learn more about this cost, which may reduce the benefits you receive, before you truly commit to a responsibility. Wagers regardless of how there is no such thing as a "no-risk" understanding, not really as one of us are denied the logical chance to bet with our saved assets. A sensible compromise lies at the place of combination of conceivable financial planning: The possibilities winning or losing are higher the more bets you place, but the possibilities winning or losing are cut down the less bets you place. However, the rigid differences between the various types of bets you contribute can be seen even when you are entrepreneurially facing two or three bet issues. Cash you place in secure stores, for instance, records bets losing regard in veritable terms (buying interest) for a really long time. This is on the grounds that there is no assurance that the paid improvement will stay aware of increasing expenses (progression). Clearly, record related hypotheses that follow the speed of progress don't conclusively in all cases follow market advance expenses. Subsequently, tolerating an augmentation might bring about lower than expected interest. Financial exchange bets are regularly expected to beat improvement and advance costs for a really long time, but you in like manner risk losing cash if costs are low when you genuinely need to sell. This could achieve a negative return, then again, cash catastrophe if costs are lower than when you purchased the thing. Right when you start monetary system, it's ordinarily smart to spread your bet by setting your money into different things and asset classes. Like that, if one theory doesn't work out as you trust, you've truly got others to get back to. When might be a great chance to begin making monetary plans? If you have immense heap of money as far as you can tell account, enough to cover you for close to three to five years, and you genuinely accept your money ought to foster after some time, you should mull over figuring out some of it. Your cash related circumstance, the conditions of your life, your capacity to bear risk, and your goals for the future will all anticipate a segment in figuring out which save resources or speculations are best for you. Being a rigid adolescent without a strong comprehension of convincing money the board is a given that it very well might be unsafe all along. The plan to ingest data of the protections trade, corresponded with the way that you're really taking a chance with your own money, is a gigantic piece of the entryway with the conceivable consequence of startling different people off considering what is genuinely one of the most reliable ways of managing controlling freedom from a worthless way of life. Key for survey even the best cash related allies started some spot, and beginning cash the pioneers and guessing that whatought to come is just every once in a while too early. As such financial creating outlines for adolescents can overpower. How you are looking at this contributing accessory is essentially a basic beginning step. In this mystery part, I'll cover all that you desire to know to spread out cash related targets, start persuading monetary fixing in withdrawal, and certification you're setting yourself up in a good way. In addition, when I first started working in the field of cash related arranging, I learned that the cash related business intentionally employs confusing language that is not entirely firmly established to denigrate the traditional monetary partner. The colossal resource managers have had the choice to run the market for a long time consequently, so we ought to focus on that they are the ones unequivocally who benefit from astounding predominantly the vast majority of us off. It is past due for a larger portion of us to devise a viable strategy for playing in their sandbox. May we at any time complete this?

CHAPTER TWO

STARTING POINTS FOR A POWERFUL MONEY MAKING GAME FOR YOUNG PEOPLE

Stage 1: Oversee Dreadful Responsibility and Avoid Money Traps in Your 40s

Take a break here and survey that I really said "stunning responsibility". Horrible commitment is obligation that you didn't require, similar to another vehicle you didn't require or a telephone overhaul you were unable to bear and put on a charge card. I'm not proposing student advances or your home credit. Enduring you have "dreadful responsibility" from Visas, you want to deal with those before you start setting assets into the cash related trade. Typically, this is fundamental.

Interest is charged on Master cards

Expecting you have a 18% financing cost on your charge card balance, you'd lose more money than you can get from attempts, even at 15% standard returns. Deal with that first so all of the cash you can place into your speculations genuinely makes you cash and keeps your cash in balance. It's in this way critical for survey that for the most part normal cash gets are not difficult to fall into. Anything you spend your got cash on that you either can't bear or don't actually have to "stay aware of the

Joneses" is a cash trap. These are things that will take all your money so you have nothing left to contribute. Before you begin convincing money related readiness, possibly of the chief concern you can do to in like manner stimulate your solitary monetary plans is to acceptably spend your cash.

Stage 2: Make an extraordinary record for the event

On the off chance that you've thought of a shrewd procedure for spending your cash, you likely likewise concocted a brilliant technique for saving it. A help stash is… you got it. a piece of your hold stays aware of that you have saved in case of an emergency. It just requires a couple of moments to put 3-6 months of your normal costs into your assist stash, which with canning essentially be a record. Along these lines, if something insane or astounding occurs, similar to a pandemic, you will be covered. Your vehicle's dialing back, an unforeseen reduction, or an amazing specialist's visit costs are examples of crises. Then again, it could similarly turn out to be useful during a trench. You'll see the value in the authentic serenity that comes from understanding that there is a pad open in the event that you truly need it, whether you truly need to benefit by your endeavor account.

Stage 3: Get to comprehend the Cash related sorting out Essentials

You wouldn't bounce into a boxing ring without knowing the vagabond pieces of doing battling and self-security, so you shouldn't weave into protections trade cash related status without understanding the wanderer pieces. It is essential to have a clear understanding of the official goal of the board's money and the communication you should use to achieve it before you can begin making financial steadfastness. At the most chief level, contributing is associated with buying $10 worth of essential worth for $5.

Right, when you are ready to buy a relationship for not precisely its genuine worth, your speculation return will foster for a really long time. This is a certain goal of strong money the load up.

Stage 4: Use Cash the board Resources for Novices

The central concern you can do to become persuading is to get contributing tutoring. The way that this is a guaranteed program shouldn't cause an excess of nervousness. Despite the posts I shared above, there are a ton of resources open weight up with experience class on my site page and on the web to zero in on the protections trade and how to win as cash related accomplice. Books, web journals, modernized convey, applications, contributing programming, and different assets are among these.

Stage 5: Make an Improvement strategy

Before you put your money watching out, you genuinely need to have a perceptible arrangement of what you truly need to accomplish and how you will get it rolling. The improvement of an improvement system becomes an integral factor here. One that is customized to your lifestyle is the most effective way to deal with progress. To get yourself situated for progress, follow the means underneath.

i. Investigate your constant monetary overabundance to pick your wagering adaptability.

ii. Last but not least, talk about your goals and how long it will take to achieve them.

iii. Pick the hypotheses and procedures that will get you to your goal the quickest and most as a matter of fact.

Having a sensible improvement system will equip you with a ton of clearness as you start reasonable cash related putting together. We should go over the third step below and look at some of the different kinds of bets you could make as another cash-related advertiser.

Step 6: Pick a Venture Type

In the accompanying part, we will examine speculation types in more prominent profundity; However, let's review some fundamental information to get you started for the time being.

Stage 7: Spread out Your Endeavor Framework

Contributing is more than picking two or three stocks and staying hopeful. If you're finishing that entire well, there's a real strategy included, and you shouldn't even worry about a hypothesis manual for get it going.

These endeavor approaches include:

i. Impact Compelling monetary preparation: Placing assets into associations that have a quantifiable normal or charitable impact

ii. Improvement Contributing: placing cash into organizations that are becoming quicker than the typical Placing assets into assurances that convey benefits

iii. Little Cap Cash the executives: putting resources into new, private companies that have the potential for quick development.

iv. Worth money management: Investing in exceptional businesses when they are being sold at prices that are lower than their true value The Standard #1 Money management system adheres to the guidelines of significant worth financial planning. Exactly when you put your money thusly, you can anyway buy improvement associations, little cap associations, and impact associations, yet you get them when they are on extraordinary. This is the principal kind of cash the board that will give you the most raised speeds of return with minimal proportion of possibility. Exactly when you buy splendid high-regard associations for half or even a fourth of their value, you can experience colossal returns.

Step 8: Sort out Where to Contribute

Whenever you've concluded your endeavor framework, you'll have to pick what stage or organization you'll use. For most monetary supporters, an electronic expert will be the best decision in light of the fact that online go-betweens grant you to put trades for a by and large little charge while at this point offering the resources in general and information you need to make wise endeavors. While you should take a gander at the costs each one charges and sort out each stage before you make your decision, you really can't end up being terrible with any of the significant web based delegates. When all is said and done, they were made to do this.

Step 9: Build a Stock Watch list

You've shown yourself and made your endeavor method, so as of now it is the ideal opportunity to start lessening your overview of potential hypotheses. If you finished up stocks are the right kind of adventure for you, you're impeccably found. Your very own stock watch list is a rundown of organizations you've investigated and viewed as beneficial ventures. At the point when you gather your watch list, you watch and trust that those associations will go set apart down. All things being equal, how might you manufacture a watch list?

PRACTICE TIRELESSNESS AND HOLD ON

Remember - at whatever point you have found an association that meets your capacities, it really may not check out to promptly take care of your money. Taking everything into account, you'll have to hang on until the stock expense is limited.

Luckily the market puts incredible associations limited continually. If you are patient, the businesses on your watch list will eventually drop to a point where you can get them at a deal rate and benefit once their prices return to their actual worth.

CONTRIBUTING TIP: TRULY CHECK YOUR SENTIMENTS OUT

Overwhelmingly, the really monetary arranging tip for beginners to follow is this: keep your emotions to yourself. If you put assets into superb associations at a second that the market has placed them on unique relative with their value, it is troublesome not to get cash; that is if you don't permit your sentiments to get the better of you. Similar to when a company is overpriced; investors often buy into it out of greed (usually because "everyone else is doing it" is reported in the news). This prompts lower returns or even disasters. On the off chance that you want to win as a monetary benefactor, you really want to do whatever it takes not to let fear or voracity drive your dynamic connection. Remain patient and steady as you contribute and you'll have the choice to avoid a critical number of the snares that beginner monetary sponsor much of the time surrender to.

Step 10: Know When to Purchase Your Stocks

Progress in individual stock financial planning is tied in with picking the perfect organizations and contributing at the ideal time, yet the ideal opportunity won't endure forever. When a company on your watch list offers a great deal, now is the time to buy. You just have to place your cash into the business now and save it there as long as possible. Your cash will see the value in incentive for a long time after you put it in the organization in the event that you made a shrewd venture.

CHAPTER THREE

INVESTING IN STOCKS FOR FLEDGLINGS

When you purchase individual shares of stock, you become a partial owner of the company's stock. This implies that you benefit too from the organization's benefits and the worth of your stocks increments with the worth of the organization. Because it enables you to profit from claiming any public corporation that you wish to put resources into, investing in stocks is without a doubt the most lucrative venture option. In general, the securities market expands at a rate of around 7% per year. However, it is possible to achieve much greater returns by investing in hand-picked individual businesses.

PLACING ASSETS INTO BONDS FOR BEGINNERS

Bonds can be purchased from the US government or from individual associations. Rather than buying ownership in an association, protections essentially license you to "credit" money to the public power or to an association as a trade-off for subtle returns. In light of everything, bonds offer an appearance of 2-3% every year.

Those benefits are noticeably flawed, especially if you're gravitating toward to retirement and don't have 40 years to foster your money. It's furthermore basic to recall that the regular speed of extension consistently is 3% or even more so you may as a matter of fact procure back the first venture.

STARTING FINANCIAL BACKERS' MANUAL FOR VENTURE SUBSIDIZES

A speculation store is a gathering of individual stocks oversaw by an asset supervisor, like common assets, ETFs, record assets, and others. While these resources are manufactured and administered by assumed "money related trained professionals", they consistently battle with beating the market when you consider the costs that save chiefs charge to regulate them for you. You'll have much less difficult time (and more horseplay) sorting out some way to take care of money in isolation, rather than relying upon some normal resource chairman who can't beat the market. Anyway, which kind of venture is best for beginners? Try not to be terrified into giving your cash to a monetary consultant or to over-broaden in an asset that will make you a similar measure of cash as it costs you by supposed "masters" or monetary counsels. It isn't our target to Approach the underlying speculation. With the right strategy, placing assets into stocks isolates to several essential standards that anyone can learn. So you shouldn't mess around with a money related specialist. Besides, this conveys us to step #7.

Contributing Tip: Practice with Paper Exchanging Paper exchanging is an extraordinary method for acquiring experience in putting away without gambling any cash. You can envision paper trading as a putting test framework as in you can exchange stocks, track your advantages and disasters, and do the wide range of various things you would do with veritable monetary arranging all while using nonexistent money. There are different electronic stages, like think or Swim, that grant you to partake in paper trading in vain so you can chip away at placing assets into the most possible sensible way without betting any veritable money.

STEP TO REWARD CONTINUE TO LEARN STRATEGIES FOR BEGINNERS

Contributing is like riding a bike, when you get its hang; it's with you for eternity. Besides, it makes you more excessive long term with the right hypothesis method. For a comprehensive look at venture types, skip ahead to the next section. We have just started to expose what's underneath here, and there is significantly more to discuss, including Cds, Home loan Upheld Protections, and the securities exchange, so you can pursue the best decision for yourself.

Various Speculations: Financial backers who are savvy know not to scatter their assets aimlessly. Taking everything into account, they emerge as OK several sorts of hypotheses and use their understanding into each to acquire cash in different ways. With respect to cash the board, there are a lot of bushels to peruse. However, it's basic to see all of your decisions before you truly set aside your money and start to create your portfolio. Each kind of adventure has its likely addition and downside. The most ideal sorts of dares to make depend upon your bet flexibility, level of appreciation of explicit business areas, course of occasions to avoid capital gains, and purposes behind placing assets into the essential spot. Among the different sorts of hypotheses out there, there are no doubt a relatively few that will work commendably for you so we ought to get into it.

CASH AND ITEMS

Cash and items are routinely seen as OK sorts of adventures, so if you're new to successful monetary preparation or are gracelessly with any bet, one of these decisions could be a respectable spot to start. Recollect that by and large safe theories furthermore will as a general rule have low returns.

1. Gold Indeed, you can place cash into gold and different items like raw petroleum or silver. Indeed, the demonstration of placing assets into gold goes way back, but that doesn't be ensured to mean it's a unimaginable endeavor. Because gold is a commodity, its value is determined by scarcity and dread, both of which can be influenced by environmental changes or political activity. Expecting you are placing assets into gold, know that your "channel" (protection from an expense drop), relies upon outside factors so the expense can sway a ton, and quickly. At the point when there is a ton of dread and shortage, the value will in general go up, yet it goes down when there is a ton of gold accessible.

Gold could be a wise speculation for you in the event that you accept that the world will turn out to be more unfortunate later on.

The most crucial point: Keep in mind that wagering on things like gold typically amounts to nothing more than wagering. It's not Rule #1 Contributing with the exception of assuming you understand that deficiency will incite an interest for gold and drive up the expense.

2. Compact discs and Bank Items Bank items are venture types offered by banks and include currency market accounts and bank accounts. Money market accounts resemble ledgers, yet routinely obtain higher credit charges as a compromise for

higher balance essentials. A Cd, or statement of store, is another kind of bank thing. Right when you purchase a Disc you agree to credit the bank a proportion of money for a doled out proportion of time to get a higher proportion of income on it than you would in a typical ledger. Discs are an exceptionally OK endeavor but with by and large protected, comes low award. The profit from Compact discs presented by most of banks is under 2% yearly, which is inadequate to stay aware of expansion.

3. Cryptographic types of cash are one of the more current kinds of adventure. They are unregulated electronic financial structures exchanged on computerized

cash destinations. Computerized types of cash, as Bitcoin or Dogecoin, have procured a lot of premium actually as an endeavor vehicle due to their quick and exciting turn of events. Regardless, they stay a certainly hazardous hypothesis because of the various dark components related with them. There is the opportunity of informal regulation and the probability that computerized cash will not at any point believe limitless affirmation to be a sort of portion. Cryptographic cash at present has no regular worth and it could disappear as quickly as it showed up.

4. U.S. Venture finances Protections and Corporate Protections, Right when you purchase any kind of safety, you are

attributing money to the substance you get it from for a fated proportion of time and premium. Because of the possibility of not receiving your money back in the event that the guarantor defaults, securities are generally regarded as safe and secure. U.S. saving protections are protections maintained by the U.S. government, which makes them almost without risk. To raise money for projects and activities, states issue securities, and partnerships that issue securities do the same. Because there is a greater risk of an organization defaulting on the credit, corporate securities are somewhat more risky than government securities. Unlike when you invest in a partnership by purchasing its stock, purchasing corporate securities does not give you ownership rights in the company. A critical note to review is that a security may simply net you a 3% benefit from your money more than quite a long while. This suggests that when you eliminate your money from the security, you'll truly have less buying influence than when you put it considering the way that the speed of improvement didn't really remain mindful of the speed of development.

5. Contract Maintained Insurances, Exactly when you purchase a home advance maintained security, you are eventually crediting money to a bank or government foundation, yet your credit is upheld by a pool of home and other land

contracts. Not by any stretch of the imagination like various bonds, which pay the head close to the completion of the bond term, contract upheld insurances pay out income and go to monetary supporters month to month. A pool of cash from numerous financial backers is utilized to make venture reserves, which are then put resources into many resources, like stocks, bonds, and different protections. The grouping of adventures conventionally tracks a market record.

6. Shared Resources, A typical resource is a sort of hypothesis store worked by a money boss who takes care of your money for you, and tries to get extraordinary returns.

Albeit shared reserves are normally included a blend of stocks and securities, in light of the fact that your cash is enhanced across various stocks and bonds, they convey less gamble. You'll simply get benefits from stock benefits and security premium, then again accepting you sell when the value of the resource goes up with the market. Concerning regard, recall that common resources are developed and regulated by assumed "money related subject matter experts" who battle with beating the market, especially when you work out the costs they're accusing you to arrangement of your money anyway.

Rule #1 Monetary benefactors expect a base yearly collected speed of return of 15% consistently or more. If we can get that, it doesn't make any difference to us what the market did considering the way that we will leave wealthy regardless.

7. Record Resources, Like normal resources, record holds are one of such corporate protections that grows your endeavor across different stocks. The qualification between record stores and normal resources is that rundown holds are idly made due, not clearly coordinated by a money boss. You have the potential for slightly better yields than with a shared asset because file reserves are latently made due, resulting in lower costs. In any

case, your benefits will be established totally on how well the rundown your resource is following does. Since most important records are used to track how the market as a whole is changing, they probably will perform as well in the long run as the market as a whole. In total, they will typically bring in an annual return of around 7%. While this isn't exactly basically as high as the benefits you can achieve through really picking individual associations with the right assessment, a decent return is fundamentally higher than the supporting expenses of a financial balance or the return speeds of securities. Exactly when you put assets into a rundown, you're fundamentally betting your money on the possible destiny of

America. You probably won't have any problems if you are confident that the American economy will continue to grow. The issue here is that expecting you put your money into a record, and we go into a slump, the market could be down for a ton of time. That suggests your portfolio will in like manner be down, and accepting at least for now that you're exorbitantly close to retirement to believe that things will swing back the other way, you could be in a tough spot. One more benefit of putting resources into individual organizations is that. The genuinely remarkable ones will by and large perform, even amidst slump.

8.	Exchange Traded Resources, Exchange Traded Resources, or ETFs as they're consistently called, resemble record funds in that they track a renowned document and mirror its display. Not by any stretch of the imagination like record holds, nonetheless, ETFs are exchanged on the protections trade. Since ETFs are traded on the protections trade, you have more control over what cost you get them at and will pay less costs. Your honor is thoroughly dependent upon how well or how ineffectually the rundown you put assets into performs. You can restrict your bet by placing assets into an ETF that tracks an extensive document, similar to the S&P 500. Simply put, investing your money in a trade-exchanged store like the S&P 500 (SPY), a list of the 500 best companies to watch, lets you take advantage of the market's growth without having to pay fees to an asset manager. While it's really smart to ask what you should place assets into, it may be essentially more basic to know what not to place assets into.

THE BEST TECHNIQUE TO PLACE ASSETS INTO BITCOIN

Also that you can exchange US Dollars for cash, for instance, Yens or Euros, you can moreover exchange your US Dollars for advanced monetary standards. Anyway computerized types of cash aren't as a matter of fact a piece of the Forex market, the mechanics of placing assets into computerized types of cash is for all intents and purposes something similar. Numerous financial backers in digital forms of money trust that the worth of those digital currencies will ascend in contrast with the dollar, and it will be moderately easy to buy them on the web. Someone who put assets into Bitcoin in 2013 and sold it today would certainly make a couple of mind blowing gains. The issue is that it's totally difficult to time the advanced currency market. The cost of Bitcoin and other digital forms of money could keep on rising essentially or tumble to nothing.

Bonds and Insurances

Bonds and insurances are various types of commonly safe endeavors. Bonds can be purchased from the US government, state and local specialists, or from individual associations. Contract upheld protections are a sort of bond that can be given by a privately owned business or by an administration office in the US.

A RESPECTABLE RULE AS A FLEDGLING IS

It's a terrible speculation on the off chance that you put large chunk of change into it and just get a lot of obligation or a lift to your confidence out of it. This consolidates expensive vehicles, lavish inner parts, and various things that decrease in regard throughout the time span you own them. While luxurious material things could help you with remaining mindful of the Jones' on your block, the benefit is ultra short lived. To have the option to bear the cost of the existence you need from now on, it's so critical to live inside your means and spend your cash admirably. Avoid these ordinary money traps and you'll have more money for the valuable things to place assets into both now and later on.

None of these are adventures, they're cash traps. Like vehicles and boats, cash sitting in a ledger is losing regard long term. Put your money into the principal kind of adventure that is guaranteed to make you cash the monetary trade.

CHAPTER FOUR

KINDS OF VENTURES ARE BEST FOR FLEDGLINGS

Everyone's reasons and individual bet versatilities are novel, so you want to decide for you which theory types suit your lifestyle, schedule, and targets best. This is just for diversion purposes, and I'm not your monetary counselor. I would do nonetheless, this:

1. To start, I would open a Roth IRA and contribute for retirement to permit my cash to develop without covering charges.

2. Then, to take care of my money with little investigation and simply drop it, I'd put a piece of it into a Record Resource,

for instance, the S&P 500 or the Russell 2000.

3. At last, but obviously not the least of these, I'd place assets into the monetary trade. We'll get into how to place assets into stocks in later segments. Regardless, it's fundamental for observe that of a great many endeavors we covered the monetary trade is the best spot to contribute with a restricted amount of money in spite of everything get gigantic returns.

How Might I Start Cash the board?

Before compelling cash the board, it is influential for extend your money related education. In this way, you want to sort out what you need to achieve and how much gamble you're willing to bring the way. Your bet changed targets will coordinate how much money you convey, the sorts of assets you buy and the length of your positions (short-, widely appealing or long stretch). When making sound financial decisions, you should take into account the following: your age; the amount and consistency of your pay; your financial goals and their time frames; your willingness to take risks. The majority of people who contribute focus on making sufficient savings for retirement. Nevertheless, numerous people do as such for additional reasons, including buying a home, starting a business, setting up young people for school and giving a legacy to loved ones. Putting your money to work through an endeavor program is an insightful strategy for achieving this huge number of targets. In any case, the technique you embrace should reflect your targets and their connected time horizons.

CONTRIBUTING TIME SKYLINES LONG VERSUS SHORT

The more market instability you can deal with, the more drawn out your mindset. A long runway empowers you to look past close term market high focuses and depressed spots and focus on long stretch execution. A venture portfolio that primarily consists of resources organized for development is reasonable in this circumstance.

The more restricted your edge of reference, the less market flimsiness you can continue on. A short runway suggests you ought to zero in on liquidity and sufficiency over improvement. A speculation portfolio that centers basically around stable-esteem, profoundly fluid resources is reasonable in this situation.

FOCAL CASH THE EXECUTIVES NORMS

Getting a theory program considering your objectives and ability to bear risk is central, yet an understanding of fundamental cash the executive's thoughts is much the same way as critical. The following depicts three major concepts. The gamble return tradeoff holds that a financial backer must accept progressively greater levels of risk in order to achieve progressively higher likely returns. On the other hand, in case a monetary patron wishes to restrict their bet receptiveness, the individual being referred to ought to disavow conceivable return. Along this continuum, there are different asset classes with unquestionable bet profiles. Essentially bet/most insignificant returning completion of the reach, you will find cash reciprocals, similar to supports of store (Albums), U.S. Store charges and widened cash market holds. You will encounter a variety of bonds with various credit characteristics, including both speculation grade and non-venture grade, as well as shifting development residencies, at a slightly higher level of risk. At the most important bet/most raised returning completion of the reach; you will find local and overall stocks. In order to achieve the ideal risk-reward tradeoff, savvy financial backers frequently keep in mind various resources for a very well-organized venture portfolio.

STREAMLINING SPECULATION EXECUTION REQUIRES EXPANSION

Right when you join different kinds of assets in a portfolio, you can deal with its capability (potential return per unit of danger anticipated). The system includes putting resources into resources that ordinarily move in uncorrelated ways and have assorted risk profiles. This suggests when one asset moves in a solitary course, others move some place startling - giving a balance in the overall portfolio. The thinking is that an enhanced portfolio will permit you to accomplish prevalent long haul returns by keeping a somewhat steady, up moving worth over the long haul.

TIME VALUE OF CASH

Financial backers must appreciate the time value of cash in addition to comprehending the gamble-reward tradeoff and the advantages of expansion. Fundamentally, this thought expresses that a dollar today is esteemed at more than a dollar tomorrow, since it can obtain income and create with time. For individuals who care about their funds, this implies trying to contribute at the earliest opportunity and as far as might be feasible. Doing so allows you to acquire by the impact of self duplicating profits and upgrades your ability to gather overflow in a segregated manner. It is crucial for spread out a good blustery day account preceding shipping off an endeavor program. For a large number individual, this infers saving six to a time of regular expenses. Taxation is always a hot topic, but when it comes to retirement, it's especially important. Charge advantaged retirement accounts. This is because the Inward Pay Organization (IRS) upholds setting something to the side for retirement by offering individuals engaging obligation benefits related with explicit hypothesis accounts, including chief upheld 401(k) plans and individual retirement accounts (IRAs). Totally sponsoring these vehicles is enthusiastically proposed by practically all financial aides. To direct life expectancy risk, which is the possibility outliving your hold reserves, experts prescribe viable cash the board 10% to 15% of gross compensation in a retirement save finances vehicle.

KINDS OF RETIREMENT RECORDS

A traditional retirement account considers charge deductions in the years responsibilities are made. During your functioning years, the commitments are contributed and permitted to develop tax-exempt. Then, in retirement, all withdrawals are charged at your continuous individual cost rate. In any case, withdrawals made before the age of 59 12 can bring about punishments, and commitments to a Roth-style retirement account can't be deducted from available pay. In light of everything, the responsibilities are contributed and allowed to foster on an obligation barred premise point forward. In retirement, all withdrawals are freed from charge assortment. Regardless, costs and disciplines can be forced on withdrawals made before the age of 59 1/2.

CHAPTER FIVE

KEY RESOURCE CLASSES

The universe of investable resources is constantly expanding, and its divisions become increasingly granular. For youngster monetary patrons, it is counterproductive to endeavor to be familiar with all of them. A more sensible strategy is to get an understanding of the essential asset classes, which are quickly summarized underneath.

Cash Reciprocals

Cash indistinguishable is a consistent worth money related instrument with an improvement of 90 days or less. As noted in advance, models consolidate smaller circles, U.S. Storehouse charges and expanded cash market holds. In comparison to other resource classes, these instruments offer unobtrusive returns and are almost entirely risk-free.

Bonds

A bond is a money related security that tends to a credit made by a monetary sponsor to a capable component. At the point when you buy a security, you are loaning cash with the assumption for getting revenue reimbursement at a foreordained future date. An exceptional case is a zero-coupon security, which includes a restricted sticker price and a particular sum portion at improvement that integrates accumulated interest and head.

Protections are intermittently given by associations, sovereign lawmaking bodies, states and neighborhood locale to finance their undertakings and extraordinary endeavors. They are typically coordinated for modestly extended terms, conventionally 5 to 10 years.

Stocks

A stock is a financial security that tends to a proportionate belonging interest in an association. The fundamental clarification a large number individual's buy stocks are to create overwhelming, long stretch hypothesis returns. This is accomplished by acknowledging cost appreciation, or the point at which a stock's price rises after it is purchased, and receiving profit installments.

Annuities

All things considered, annuities are not hypothesis instruments. They are security things that include frank purchases as a trade-off for a movement of brief or surrendered pay transports, which can be changed - in regards to measure, timing, vacillation and term. Typical sorts of annuities consolidate fixed annuities, recorded annuities and variable annuities. Since they give consistent, dependable loan costs, fixed annuities are the most reliable of the three. Because their profits can change, ordered annuities are noticeably more risky. Variable annuities are the most dangerous sort of annuity, since they include tolerating hypothesis positions in stocks and bonds.

Help with Investments

There is a lot to learn when you first start investing. To be sure, even the savviest monetary supporters have data openings, given continuously progressing macroeconomic speculations, new financial things, charge guideline changes and other managerial developments. Fortunately, you don't have to investigate this multifaceted design isolated. Think about working with a financial advisor who is a fiduciary. Lawfully and ethically, these credentialed monetary experts promise to constantly act to the greatest advantage of their clients. Regardless, their organizations incorporate a few significant inconveniences, but the expert course and informative benefit they give can be significant, especially, for juvenile monetary sponsor. According to Cheng, "For our clients, we address both a drawn out money management plan for their life monetary objectives and transient reserve funds for any crises or open doors that emerge." They can abstain from pursuing close to home choices in regards to their ventures along these lines, which gives them genuine serenity.

Other Warning Choices For New Financial backers, Full-Administration Monetary Counsels Aren't the Main Wellspring of

Help If you are good with development and have a confined proportion of money to contribute, using a robo-specialist or a scaled down cash the executives application could be sensible (and functional).

STAGES FOR ROBO-WARNING

A robo-counselor is a mechanized venture the board administration that utilizes simulated intelligence controlled calculations and inside and out internet based polls to decide your gamble resistance and make and keep a fitting speculation portfolio. Progression, Wealthfront and Ellevest are notable plans.

Smaller than usual cash the board Applications

A small monetary arranging application is a kind of robo-expert that grants you to place cash in minuscule expansions. Supporting techniques change. Some small cash the board applications assemble purchases made through associated Visas or charge cards and hoard investable resources for you. Others consider finance inferences and intermittent trades from your checking or speculation accounts. Reserve and oak seeds are two notable small contributing applications you might want to think about.

THE END